A Note to Parents

DK READERS is a compelling program for beginning readers, designed in conjunction with leading literacy experts.

Beautiful illustrations and superb full-color photographs combine with engaging, easy-to-read stories to offer a fresh approach to each subject in the series. Each DK READER is guaranteed to capture a child's interest while developing his or her reading skills, general knowledge, and love of reading.

The four levels of DK READERS are aimed at different reading abilities, enabling you to choose the books that are exactly right for your child:

Level 1 – Beginning to read
Level 2 – Beginning to read alone
Level 3 – Reading alone
Level 4 – Proficient readers

The "normal" age at which a child begins to read can be anywhere from three to eight years old, so these levels are only a general guideline.

No matter which level you select, you can be sure that you are helping your child learn to read, then read to learn!

LONDON, NEW YORK, MELBOURNE,
MUNICH, AND DELHI

Editor Kate Phelps
Designer Sooz Bellerby
Series Editor Alastair Dougall
Production Nicola Torode
Picture Researcher Jo de Gray
Picture Library Rose Horridge

First American Edition, 2003
03 04 05 06 07 10 9 8 7 6 5 4 3 2 1
Published in the United States by DK Publishing, Inc.
375 Hudson Street, New York, New York 10014

Library of Congress Cataloging-in-Publication Data

Gaff, Jackie.
 Superman's guide to the universe / written by Jackie Gaff.-- 1st
American ed.
 p. cm. -- (DK readers)
Summary: Superman invites the reader to fly along with him as he
explores and explains the universe.
Includes index.
 ISBN 0-7894-9746-8 -- ISBN 0-7894-9754-9 (pbk.)
 1. Astronomy--Juvenile literature. 2. Cosmology--Juvenile literature.
[1. Astronomy. 2. Cosmology.] I. Title. II. Series: Dorling Kindersley
readers.
 QB46.G26 2003
 523.1--dc21
                            2003004920

Color reproduction by Media Development and Printing Ltd, UK
Printed and bound in China by L Rex Printing Co., Ltd.

The publisher thanks the following for their kind permission
to reproduce their photographs:
c=center; t=top; b=below; l=left; r=right

Cover Anglo Australian Observatory; 5 NASA: bc; 9 NASA: c; 11 NASA: bc; 13 NASA: tc; 15
NASA: tr; 18 London Planetarium: tl; 19 NASA: c, SPL: Novosti tr; 20 NASA: bc; 21 NASA/JPL; 23
SPL: Science, Industry & Business Library/New York Public Library br; 24 London Planetarium: tl; 25
NASA: br, NASA/JPL: tc; 27 NASA, NASA/JPL: tc; 29 SPL: George Bernard tr; 31 NASA: tc; 33
NASA/JPL: tc; 35 Anglo Australian Observatory: cb, Anglo Australian Observatory: tc; 37 NASA:
tc; 40 SPL: Space Telescope Science Institute tl; 41 NASA: tc; 43 NASA: JPL tc, SPL: David Parker
cr, SPL: Victor Habbick Visions bc; 44 SPL: Mark Garlick bc; 47 NASA: bc.

All other photographs © Dorling Kindersley.
For further information see: www.dkimages.com

Dorling Kindersley would like to thank the following artists for their contribution to this book:
Marlo Alquiza, Jon Bogdanove, John Byrne, James Calafiore, Andrew Chiu, John Dell,
Dale Eaglesham, George Freeman, Ron Frenz, Dick Giordano, Tom Grummet, Andrew Hennessy,
John Holdredge, Stuart Immonen, Georges Jeanty, Dave Johnson, Jeff Johnson, Andy Lanning,
Doug Mahnke, Jason Martin, Kenny Martinez, José Marzan, John McCrea, Ed McGuinness,
Mark McKenna, Mike McKone, Jaime Mendoza, Mark Millar, Paul Neary, Tom Nguyen,
Jerry Ordway, Howard Porter, Pablo Raimondi, Rodney Ramos, Cliff Rathburn, Darick Robertson,
Denis Rodier, Hanibal Rodriguez, Duncan Rouleau, Paul Ryan, Joe Shuster, Bill Sienkiewicz,
Cam Smith, Dexter Vines, Mike Wieringo, Anthony Williams, Walden Wong

Discover more at
www.dk.com

Contents

DK READERS

PROFICIENT
4
READERS

JLA SUPERMAN'S GUIDE TO THE UNIVERSE

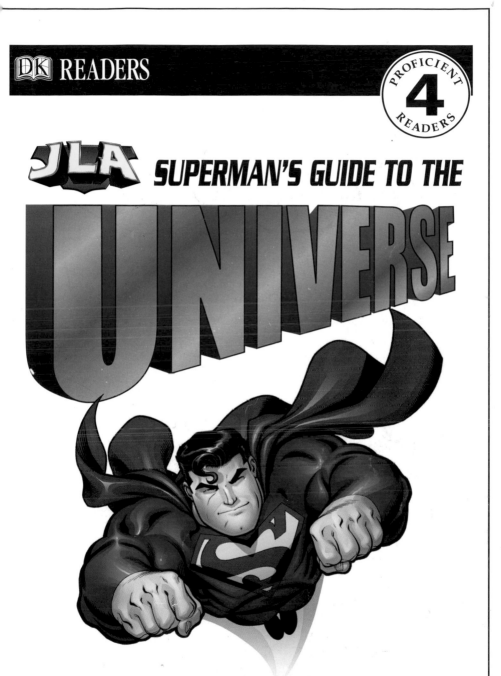

Written by Jackie Gaff

Superman created by Jerry Siegel and Joe Shuster

DK

Amazing space

Welcome on board, Earthling, for the trip of a lifetime. Launch yourself into space and fly with me, Superman, on a sensational exploration of the Universe!

Prepare yourself for a long flight, because the Universe is unbelievably big—if it were the size of the Pacific Ocean, the Sun would be smaller than a grain of sand!

We're going everywhere, so hang on tight. The Universe is space and everything in it—you, your friends, your family, and everything else on planet Earth. It's the Earth itself and the other planets, plus Earth's moon and all the other planets' moons. Our star, the

Comic debut
The Man of Steel made his first appearance in *Action Comics* in June 1938. Also making their debuts were Clark Kent and Lois Lane.

Sun and all the stars you can see in the night sky are part of the Universe, too. Don't forget, there are billions and billions more stars you can't see because they are too far away.

Are you ready for the journey of a lifetime? Up, up, and away!

Several hundred never-before-seen galaxies are visible in this view of the Universe, taken by the Hubble Space Telescope. Hubble is a satellite telescope that orbits Earth.

"S" symbol
Superman's emblem has its origins in a Native American blanket that belonged to the Kents' ancestors. The "S" represents a snake.

Time travel
The deeper we look into space, the farther back we look in time. This is because starlight takes time to cross the vast distances of space to reach our eyes.

Narrow escape
Just seconds before a cataclysmic explosion destroyed their home planet of Krypton, Superman's parents, Jor-El and Lara Lor-Van, launched their baby in a spacecraft toward Earth.

Family circle

The planet Earth belongs to a family of nine planets that travel around a star, the Sun. From nearest to farthest from the Sun, the nine planets are: Mercury, Venus, Earth, Mars, Jupiter, Saturn, Uranus, Neptune, and Pluto. The Sun together with the planets, their moons, and all the other space bodies that travel around the Sun make up the Solar System—"solar" means "of the Sun."

The path of a space body around the Sun is called an orbit. Each of the nine planets orbits the Sun at a different speed, and the planets are all traveling incredibly quickly—Earth, for instance, is speeding around the Sun at almost 68,500 mph (110,000 km/h). The time that Earth takes for a single orbit is called a year.

But that's not the only way the planets are moving. Each planet is also rotating, or turning around. The planets rotate at different speeds, and as each one turns around, different areas move into and out of the Sun's heat and light. The areas facing the Sun have daylight, while those facing away have the darkness of night. A day is the time from sunrise to sunrise, and on Earth, it lasts 24 hours.

Happy landing
The superbaby's spacecraft fell to Earth near Smallville, in Kansas, where it was found by farmers Martha and Jonathan Kent. They decided to raise the boy as their own son.

The JLA
Earth is protected by the Justice League of America. The super heroes are (clockwise from top) J'onn J'onzz, Superman, Green Lantern, Batman, Aquaman, Wonder Woman, the Flash, and Plastic Man.

The living planet

Earth is unique—the only planet in the Solar System known to have living things. The chief reason why life on Earth is possible is that it is the only planet to have liquid water on its surface. There are millions of different creatures and plants on Earth, but they all have one thing in common. None would survive without water. Earth is in the Sun's life zone—just the right distance away for liquid water and, therefore, life to be possible. All Earth's water would have boiled away if it were too close to the Sun's heat. If it were too far away from the Sun, the water would be locked away as ice.

There is another reason why life exists on Earth—its atmosphere, the skin of gases around it. This protects Earth from the Sun's harmful rays and contains the gases that most animals and plants need to breathe.

Ocean king Superman's fellow JLA member, Aquaman, safeguards Earth's oceans from his home city of Poseidonis, deep beneath the Atlantic waves.

EARTH: VITAL STATISTICS
Diameter: 7,926 miles (12,756 km)
Average surface temperature: 59°F (15°C)
Length of a day (sunrise to sunrise): 24 Earth hours
Length of a year: 365.25 Earth days
Distance from the Sun: 93 million miles (150 million km)

Earth looks blue from space because nearly three-quarters of its surface is covered by vast oceans of liquid water. In the lowest layer of the atmosphere, winds blow clouds and weather around the planet.

The Moon

Earth's nearest neighbor in space is the Moon, and it's the only place beyond Earth that humans have visited. The first men to walk on the Moon were American astronauts Neil Armstrong and Buzz Aldrin, on July 21, 1969. Only 10 other men have been lucky enough to follow in their footsteps, the last in 1972.

Moons are space bodies that orbit a planet, and most of the planets have them. Earth only has

Sea of Serenity

Lunar world
The surface of the Moon is pocked with craters, caused by space rocks bombarding it. There are also mountain ranges and wide plains known as "seas."

Heavenly HQ
The HQ of Earth's super-powered protectors, the JLA, is a fortress on the Moon. It's called the Watchtower and is in the Sea of Serenity.

one, but the record-holder, Jupiter, has an astonishing 60 or more of them!

The Moon is roughly a quarter the size of Earth and about 239,000 miles (384,500 km) away. Its orbit of Earth takes just over 27 days.

League matters
The JLA meets on the Moon to discuss any threats to Earth.

Buzz Aldrin walks on the Moon in July, 1969 during the first-ever Moon landing. The photograph was taken by fellow astronaut Neil Armstrong.

HOW MANY MOONS?

Mercury	0
Venus	0
Earth	1
Mars	2
Jupiter	60
Saturn	31
Uranus	21
Neptune	11
Pluto	1

Hot stuff

At 109 times the size of Earth, the Sun is unimaginably huge. It is also immensely hot. Even the coolest part, its surface, is 9,900°F (5,500°C)—hot enough not just to melt iron, but to make it boil away in a puff of gas.

Unlike the planets, whose cores are made of rock or metal, stars are made only of gas. The Sun is fueled by hydrogen gas, as are most other stars. It's like a gigantic power station, generating enormous amounts of heat and light.

All this energy is produced in the Sun's center, or core, where temperatures reach an astonishing 27 million°F (15 million°C). Conditions in the core are so extreme that atoms of hydrogen gas join together to form helium gas. This process is called nuclear fusion,

Sun lover
Superman's superpowers are fueled by the effect of the Sun's rays on his Kryptonian body cells.

Tyrant sun
The JLA fought and conquered Solaris, an evil artificial star from a future time.

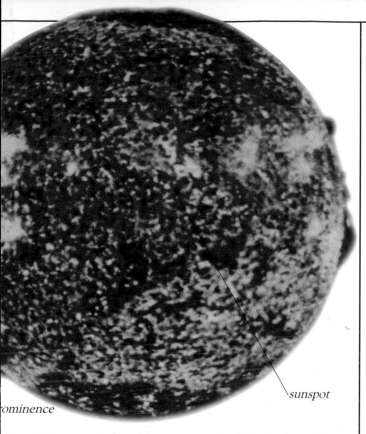

sunspot

prominence

Just 0.15 square inches (one square cm) of the Sun's surface shine as brightly as 230,000 candles.

Watch out!
The Sun's rays are powerful enough to damage your eyes or even cause blindness, so never look directly at the Sun, even when wearing sunglasses. Never, ever look at the Sun through binoculars or a telescope.

Golden globe
The Sun's surface is called the photosphere. The core is where the Sun's energy is produced.

and it generates all the energy the Sun needs to keep shining.

The Sun's surface is dotted with dark patches called sunspots. These areas are about 2,700°F (1,500°C) cooler than the rest of the Sun's surface. Prominences are gigantic fountains of glowing gas that shoot out into space from the surface of the Sun.

core

photosphere

13

Invisible glue

An invisible force keeps things on Earth and stops them from floating off into space. It's called gravity, and it's so powerful that to escape its pull and blast off into space, rockets have to travel at over 7 miles (11 km) per second!

Everything in the Universe has gravity, however, not just Earth. Gravity is the invisible glue that holds the Universe together.

An object's mass is the amount of matter, or material, it is made of, and the greater an object's mass, the stronger its gravity.

Earth's gravity not only keeps people's feet on the ground, but it also holds the Moon in

Superlight flight
As Earth's gravity is weaker than that of Superman's home planet, Krypton, its pulling effect on Superman's Kryptonian body is weaker. That's one reason why he's able to fly.

Superman didn't realize he could fly until his late teens, when his dog Rusty accidentally knocked him into a deep ravine.

14

orbit around Earth. At 28 times the strength of Earth's, the Sun's gravity is powerful enough to hold all the other space bodies in the Solar System in orbit around it.

When a spacecraft orbits Earth, it is actually falling toward the planet's surface, pulled by its gravity. The spacecraft manages to stay out in orbit because it's traveling so fast that it only falls as much as Earth's surface curves beneath it.

Floating feeling
The astronauts in and around an orbiting spacecraft are falling, too. This makes them float about and seem weightless.

SURFACE GRAVITY
(in comparison to Earth, which = 1)

Sun	28
Mercury	0.38
Venus	0.91
Earth	1
Mars	0.38
Jupiter	2.36
Saturn	0.92
Uranus	0.89
Neptune	1.12
Pluto	0.06

Gravity beaters
Kryptonian scientists invented an anti-gravity generator to lift and propel their futuristic flyer pods.

Mysterious Mercury

The closest planet to the Sun, Mercury is only slightly larger than our Moon. It looks similar to the Moon, too, with its surface pockmarked by thousands of craters made by space rocks crashing into the planet.

Mercury has almost no atmosphere. That means that there's nothing to protect it from the Sun's fierce heat during the daytime or to hold in warmth after darkness falls. And a day is very very long on Mercury. Sunrise to sunrise lasts just under six Earth months.

Although Mercury's days are long, its year is the shortest in the entire Solar System. The planet is so close to the Sun, and orbiting so quickly, that its year lasts about three Earth months.

Breath of air
There's no air in space, and although Superman can hold his breath for a super-long time, for extra-long journeys he sometimes wears a high-tech oxygen mask.

Brainy back-up
Superman's oxygen mask was invented by technological genius Professor Emil Hamilton.

Almost everything we know about Mercury came from the US spacecraft *Mariner 10*, which flew past the planet in the 1970s and took close-up photographs.

mantle   crust

core

Mercury's cratered surface.

The rocky planets

Mercury, Venus, Earth and Mars are mainly made of rock and metal. Each has an outer layer called a crust that is solid rock. A layer of molten rock, called the mantle, is underneath. The rocky planets' cores are made of solid metal.

MERCURY: VITAL STATISTICS

Diameter: 4,879 km (3,032 miles)

Average surface temperature: 167°C (333°F)

Length of a day (sunrise to sunrise): 176 Earth days

Length of a year: 88 Earth days

Distance from the Sun: 58 million km (36 million miles)

US spacecraft Mariner 10.

Venomous Venus

Landing on Venus would be like touching down in hell! It may not be the closest planet to the Sun, but it's the hottest place in the Solar System, with temperatures soaring as high as 900°F (475°C)—the Sahara Desert, the hottest place on Earth, only reaches about 150°F (66°C).

Venus gets so hot because, unlike Mercury, it has an atmosphere. This is mainly made of a gas called carbon dioxide that acts like a big heavy blanket, trapping in heat and turning the planet into an oven.

But that's not all. Venus's clouds are made of deadly sulphuric acid, while its atmosphere pushes down on the planet's surface with 92 times the pressure of Earth's. This means that anything unlucky enough to land on its surface would be crushed within minutes!

Venus is almost the same size as Earth.

Armor plating
When the going gets tough, JLA ally John Henry Irons (Steel) protects his body by donning super-strong armor.

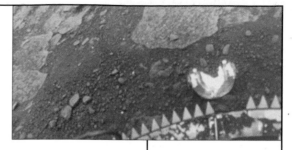

The planet Venus is the brightest object in the night sky after the Moon, and it is clearly visible from Earth with the naked eye. It's best seen just after sunset (look to the west) or before dawn (look to the east).

Space invaders
A series of Soviet *Venera* spacecraft visited Venus and sent robot landers to its surface in the 1960s to 1980s.

Venus is covered in volcanoes, some of which are higher than Mount Everest. Scientists aren't sure whether the volcanoes are still active.

Man of Steel
Superman's Kryptonian body is protected by an invisible force field. Even bullets just bounce off him.

VENUS: VITAL STATISTICS
Diameter: 7,521 miles (12,104 km)
Average surface temperature: 867°F (464°C)
Length of a day (sunrise to sunrise): 117 Earth days
Length of a year: 225 Earth days
Distance from the Sun: 67 million miles (108 million km)

Mars, the red planet

For centuries, people thought that life might exist on Mars. As recently as the last century, science-fiction writers were populating it with little green men.

Humans got their first chance to investigate the planet's surface in 1976, when two US *Viking* spacecrafts sent down robot landers. Then, in 1997, the US *Pathfinder* mission used a robot buggy called *Sojourner* to rove across the landscape analyzing the rock.

Martian Manhunter
Superman's fellow JLA member, the green-skinned J'onn J'onzz, is the sole survivor of a plague that wiped out the rest of his kind.

This robot buggy, called Sojourner, *was sent to explore the surface of Mars.*

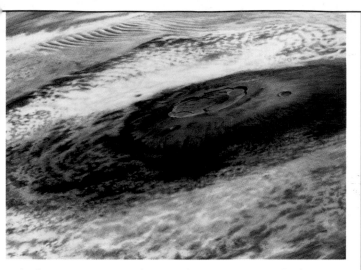

The biggest Martian volcano, Olympus Mons, is the largest in the Solar System. At 16 miles (27 km) high, it's three times taller than Mount Everest!

Mission to Mars
Scientists hope to send human explorers to Mars one day. It'll take them a long time to get there, though—the one-way trip takes at least six months.

No signs of life have been discovered, although scientists hope that future missions may yet find traces of tiny bacteria or algae. This is because there is evidence that liquid water once flowed across the Martian landscape. None remains today, but Mars still has some frozen water in its polar regions.

MARS: VITAL STATISTICS
Diameter: 4,222 miles (6,794 km)
Average surface temperature: –85°F (–65°C)
Length of a day (sunrise to sunrise): 25 Earth hours
Length of a year: 1.9 Earth years
Distance from the Sun: 142 million miles (228 million km)

Alien alert
The White Martians are an evil race, determined to conquer Earth.

Astonishing asteroids

Orbiting the Sun between Mars and Jupiter is a belt of billions of chunks of space rock. The smallest are just a few feet (meters) wide, but, at 580 miles (930 km) across, the largest, Ceres, is about a quarter the size of the Moon. These space rocks are called asteroids.

Most, but not all, asteroids lie in this belt. Some have broken free and follow their own individual orbits around the Sun. Sometimes their orbits bring them close to Earth, and scientists call these rogue rocks Near Earth Asteroids (NEAs for short).

From time to time, Earth is hit by an NEA.

Hot stuff
When an asteroid threatened Earth, Superman and Green Lantern used their superpowers to blast the rock into oblivion.

When the JLA defeated the General, they teleported the monster to a rock in the Asteroid Belt.

This illustration shows the Asteroid Belt, which orbits the Sun between Mars and Jupiter.

Most are small and plunge harmlessly into the ocean, but scientists are using space telescopes to keep an eye out for any dangerously large ones. If a big NEA is found to be heading for Earth, scientists hope to use missiles or lasers to push the NEA off course long before it hits, so don't panic!

Some asteroids contain huge amounts of valuable metals, such as iron, nickel, cobalt, and copper. One day it may be possible to send spacecraft to NEAs to mine these precious materials.

Shooting stars
Earth is under constant bombardment from space dust and pebbles. Most of this space rubble burns up in the atmosphere, creating streaks of light as it falls. These are meteors, or shooting stars.

Gigantic Jupiter

The fifth planet from the Sun, Jupiter, is the biggest in the Solar System—more than two and half times as massive as all the other planets combined!

Jupiter is the record holder in more ways than one, because it also has the greatest number of moons. Most of its 60 moons are tiny, but its largest moon, Ganymede, is the biggest moon in the Solar System. At a massive 3,272 miles (5,268 km) across, it's larger than the planet Mercury.

Jupiter is also the fastest-spinning of all the planets, rotating once every 10 Earth hours. It is Jupiter's speed that pulls its clouds out into the bands that pattern its surface.

The beautiful patterns on Jupiter's surface are created by swirling bands of clouds.

Secret hero
Daily Planet reporter Clark Kent hides a secret. He is really the Man of Steel, ready when duty calls to transform into Superman!

Jupiter's Great Red Spot is a storm three times as big as Earth that has been raging for more than 300 years.

Watery worlds
Jupiter's two largest moons, Ganymede and Callisto, seem to have a solid crust of rock and ice, while its fourth largest, Europa, is covered in cracked ice.

World of lava
Jupiter's third largest moon, Io, is a mass of erupting volcanoes. Lava on its surface makes it look like a huge, moldy orange!

There's no way that we could land on Jupiter to explore it, though, because it doesn't have a solid crust. Along with Saturn, Uranus, and Neptune, Jupiter's outer layer is a gassy atmosphere, with liquid gas beneath and a small rocky core.

JUPITER: VITAL STATISTICS
Diameter: 88,846 miles (142,984 km)
Average cloud-top temperature: −166°F (−110°C)
Length of a day (sunrise to sunrise): 10 Earth hours
Length of a year: 11.9 Earth years
Distance from the Sun: 484 million miles (779 million km)

25

Spectacular Saturn

All four gas giants, Saturn, Uranus, Neptune, and Jupiter, are braceleted by rings made up of millions of chunks of icy rock, ranging from pebble-sized to boulders as big as houses. The widest and most spectacular of these rings belong to Saturn. They glitter and gleam in the Sun's light and are bright enough to be seen from Earth through good binoculars.

Saturn is the second largest planet in the Solar System, but it's also the least dense. In fact, it's light enough to float in water if you could find a big enough bucket!

All aboard
Apart from Superman, only a few JLA members can fly, let alone travel through space. When it comes to interplanetary travel, these nonflying super heroes usually hop on board a supersleek jump shuttle.

Many of the JLA's high-tech gadgets are dreamed up by the scientists who work in the US government's S.T.A.R. Labs.

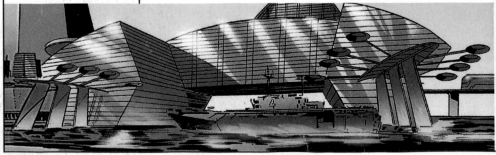

The gas giant Saturn and its incredible rings.

Saturn's rings are 62,000 miles (100,000 km) wide but are less than 0.6 miles (1 km) thick.

The *Cassini-Huygens* spacecraft is due to reach Saturn and its moons in 2004, after a seven-year journey. Scientists are eager to study Saturn's largest moon, Titan, because it is the only moon in the Solar System with its own thick atmosphere.

The JLA uses a teleporter to bring equipment and supplies to its base on the Moon.

SATURN: VITAL STATISTICS

Diameter: 74,897 miles (120,536 km)

Average cloud-top temperature: −220°F (−140°C)

Length of a day (sunrise to sunrise): 11 Earth hours

Length of a year: 29.5 Earth years

Distance from the Sun: 891 million miles (1,434 million km)

Unusual Uranus

There's something very strange about Uranus. Unlike all the other planets, it rotates on its side, at right angles to its orbit around the Sun. This makes the warmest place on Uranus its poles!

All of Uranus's 21 moons are also lying on their sides. At just 300 miles (480 km) across, its largest moon, Miranda, is about one-seventh the size of Earth's moon.

Like the three other giant planets, Uranus has rings and is mainly made of gas. Its beautiful green color comes from the gas methane in its atmosphere.

The planets Mercury, Venus, Mars, Jupiter, and

Scientists think that a collision with a gigantic space rock billions of years ago may have pushed Uranus on its side.

Emerald warrior
One of the younger members of the JLA is Green Lantern Kyle Rayner, owner of the willpower-controlled Power Ring.

Herschel constructed this large telescope in 1787–89.

Saturn can all be seen from Earth with the naked eye and have been known since ancient times. Uranus, Neptune, and Pluto can only be seen through a telescope and weren't known until long after its invention. Uranus was the first planet to be discovered through a telescope, in 1781 by the astronomer William Herschel. He built his own telescopes and later discovered two of Uranus's moons.

URANUS: VITAL STATISTICS
Diameter: 31,763 miles (51,118 km)
Average cloud-top temperature: −319°F (−195°C)
Length of a day (sunrise to sunrise): 17 Earth hours
Length of a year: 83.8 Earth years
Distance from the Sun: 1,785 million miles (2,873 million km)

Green menace
The color green has a special link with Superman. It is the color of kryptonite. The deadly radiation given off by these fragments from Superman's home planet can poison the Man of Steel.

Stormy Neptune

Neptune is similar in size and color to its neighbor Uranus, although bluer.

Super-speedster
What's speedier than the winds on Neptune? Superman, of course! No one knows exactly how fast he can fly, but his top speed is near the speed of light—nearly 186,000 miles (300,000 km) per second!

Howling windstorms rage through the atmospheres of all four giant planets, but the roughest weather of all belongs to Neptune. Winds tear across its surface at speeds of up to 1,250 mph (2,000 km/h)—more than four times faster than in the worst tornado ever recorded on Earth.

Astronomers discovered the planet Neptune before 1846, when they first saw it through a telescope. They had predicted its position using math, after they realized that neighboring Uranus's orbit was being affected by an unknown object's gravity.

The spacecraft
Voyager 2 *produced
this image of Triton
during its close flyby
on August 25, 1989.*

Eleven moons have so far been discovered around Neptune, and its largest, Triton, has a very odd habit—it orbits the planet backward. That's not the only strange thing about Triton. It's one of the coldest places in the Solar System and has active volcanoes that spit out ice!

Greased lightning
Another of the JLA's super-powered speedsters is the Flash (Wally West). Powered by the Speed Force, he's also able to run at near light-speed.

EPTUNE: VITAL STATISTICS
ameter: 30,775 miles (49,528 km)
verage cloud-top temperature: −328°F (−200 °C)
ngth of a day (sunrise to sunrise): 16 Earth hours
ngth of a year: 164.8 Earth years
stance from the Sun: 2,794 million miles (4,496 million km)

31

Puzzling Pluto

At one-fifth Earth's size, the farthest planet from the Sun, Pluto, is also the smallest. With an average surface temperature of –373°F (–225°C), it's also the coldest planet. Unlike Neptune and the other three giant planets, Pluto is a solid ball of rock and ice.

In fact, some scientists think that Pluto isn't a planet at all, but one of the space bodies they call ice dwarfs. Ice dwarfs are similar to asteroids, but instead of being solid rock, they are a mixture of rock, water ice, and other frozen chemicals. Thousands of ice dwarfs are thought to orbit the Sun beyond Neptune, in a region known as the Edgeworth-Kuiper Belt.

Pluto was the last planet in the Solar System to be discovered, by American astronomer

Pluto is just two-thirds the size of Earth's Moon.

Ice bound
When Superman wants to cool villains down, he doesn't need to exile them to chilly Pluto. A single gust of his flash-freezing breath is enough!

Space snowballs
Comets are lumps of snow and dust that usually orbit the Sun in and beyond the Edgeworth-Kuiper Belt. Some comets, however, break free and speed through space toward the Sun. As a comet nears the Sun, the heat makes the snow turn to gas, which streams out behind it in two tails.

Clyde Tombaugh in 1930. No spacecraft has ever visited it, but scientists hope to launch a mission to investigate it in 2006. The spacecraft should reach Pluto by 2015 and the Edgeworth-Kuiper Belt about 10 years later.

PLUTO: VITAL STATISTICS
Diameter: 1,485 miles (2,390 km)
Average surface temperature: –373°F (–225°C)
Length of a day (sunrise to sunrise): 6.4 Earth days
Length of a year: 248 Earth days
Distance from the Sun : 3,647 million miles (5,870 million km)

The Milky Way

The Key
The goal of chemically enhanced supervillain the Key is to rule reality. The JLA has so far managed to stop him.

Just as Earth is one of a family of planets, so the Sun belongs to a star family called a galaxy. The Sun is in the galaxy we call the Milky Way—it was named by the ancient Greeks, who thought it looked like milk streaming from the breast of their goddess Hera.

Galaxies are like islands of stars in the vast ocean of the Universe. There are billions of galaxies, each containing millions upon millions of stars.

Distances in space are so huge that scientists measure them in light-years, the distance light travels in one year—5.9 million million miles (9.5 million million km). The Milky Way Galaxy measures 100,000 light-years across and is 4,000 light-years thick. It is shaped like an enormous bulging

An irregular galaxy.

An elliptical galaxy.

Galaxies galore
Not all galaxies are the same shape. Some are spiral-shaped like the Milky Way. Other galaxies are irregular (with no particular shape) or elliptical (ball-and egg-shaped).

Alien star
Starro was a starfish-shaped alien from another galaxy who tried to enslave the population of Earth until stopped by the JLA.

disk with long spiraling arms, and it contains an astonishing 500 billion stars—far too many to think about, let alone count!

The young stars that scientists call protostars.

Tiny titan
An experiment with the fallen fragment of a white dwarf star helped physics professor Ray Palmer shrink his body and begin battling crime as the Atom!

A Universe of stars

The stars may all look alike when you gaze into the night sky. But if you could get closer to those twinkling lights, you'd see that they come in all sizes and colors.

The biggest stars are the giants and supergiants—a red giant can be 10 times the size of the Sun, while a supergiant can be 10 times the size of a red giant. There are smaller stars than the Sun, too. White dwarfs can be Earth-sized, while the smallest stars, neutron stars, are the size of a big city.

All stars are born, shine for a time, and then die. The Sun is a medium-sized, middle-aged star. It was born about five billion years ago and has enough gas fuel left to last another five billion or so. It will then start to die.

Dark pillars of a nebula's gas, photographed by the Hubble Space Telescope.

Stars are born inside vast clouds of gas and dust called nebulae. Inside each nebula, gravity pulls gas into ever denser, ever hotter balls, which eventually start to spin and glow. These young stars are called protostars. They get hotter and hotter until they shine steadily, as true stars.

Shaping up
Patterns of stars in the sky are known as constellations. They are often named after a mythological creature or person, such as Orion.

The Sun is a type of star known as a yellow dwarf. Here, other types of star are shown in relation to a yellow dwarf.

yellow dwarf

giant star

white dwarf

neutron

ergiant

Star death

Most stars start to die when the hydrogen gas fuel in their core runs low. Stars like the Sun then slowly swell into a red giant. Eventually, the red giant's outer layers are puffed off into space, while its core collapses in on itself to become a white dwarf star— thousands of times smaller than the red giant but still very hot. It takes

Superman Red

All change
When the Sun was consumed by "Sun-Eater," Superman lost his powers. Attempts to restore them caused him to split into Superman Red and Blue.

1. A massive blue-white giant star begins to die.

2. It swells and changes color, turning yellow then red.

3. It balloons into a supergiant star 100s of times bigger than the Sun before going supernova.

A supernova explosion.

billions of years for the star to cool and fade to a cinder.

Some more massive stars than the Sun have a far more dramatic ending. This kind of star swells into a supergiant before blasting itself apart in a vast flash of light called a supernova. A supernova is one of the brightest objects in the whole Universe—giving off as much light as all the stars in an entire galaxy combined.

Superman Blue

A Hubble Space Telescope image of a whirlpool of hot gas fueling a suspected black hole.

Spaghetti junction
If an astronaut fell into a black hole, its gravity would pull so hard that his or her body would be stretched out like spaghetti!

Black holes

When a star goes supernova, its core collapses in on itself and is pulled tighter and tighter and smaller and smaller by gravity. The dying star's core may end as a tiny neutron star. Sometimes, though, a neutron star carries on shrinking and becomes a black hole.

Black holes are among space's biggest mysteries. Their gravity is so powerful that it sucks in anything that comes near. Even light cannot escape—that's why the "holes" are described as black. Because our eyes cannot see without light, finding a black hole in the blackness of space is very difficult. Scientists do it not by looking directly at them but by detecting their effect on a nearby

Stars that come in pairs are called binary stars. If one of the pair has collapsed into a black hole, it may be sucking in gas from its companion star.

star. The telltale signs are the invisible X-rays that are given off as a black hole's super-strong gravity hoovers up the star's gas. The gas spins around the black hole like a whirlpool, becoming extremely hot—up to 180 million°F (100 million°C)—and making it give off X-rays.

Rising pulse
A pulsar is a neutron star that spins rapidly, giving off pulses of radiation.

A pulsar.

Supersight
One of Superman's powers is his X-ray vision. It allows him to see through all solid materials, apart from lead.

Otherworldly
Superman's enemies are not limited to Earth creatures. General Zod is a formidable alien foe, who is intent on world domination.

Superman and the alien Massacre trade blows.

Is anyone out there?

Are we alone in the Universe or are there aliens somewhere out there? An alien life-form might be anything from a tiny bacteria to an intelligent being, but one thing is certain—there's no scientific proof that any kind of alien exists, let alone creatures capable of inventing spacecraft that can travel across the vastness of space to visit Earth.

Scientists have proved, however, that there are other stars apart from the Sun with planets. Since the first was detected in the early 1990s, more than 100 planets have been found outside the Solar System.

One day a planet may be discovered that's in its star's life zone—with the liquid water needed to make life possible!

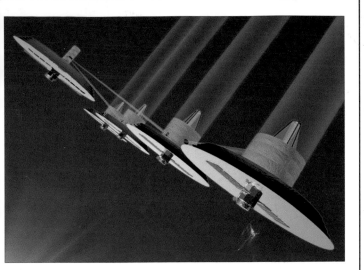

Scientists are coming up with ideas for new spacecraft all the time. This illustration shows one idea—a spacecraft that will carry telescopes powerful enough to detect faraway planets.

The SETI@home website is at http://setiathome. berkeley.edu

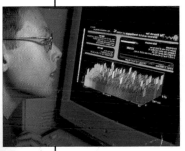

SETI

Scientists are using radio telescopes to listen out for radio signals broadcast by aliens. This program is known as SETI (the Search for ExtraTerrestrial Intelligence).

Some people say they have been abducted by aliens. The extraterrestrials are often described as little green or gray men.

Interstellar travel

Even if humans were to make contact with an alien civilization, they don't have the technology to visit another solar system. The stars are just too far away.

The closest star to the Sun, Proxima Centauri, is 4.3 light-years away. Traveling in the space shuttle at 17,000 mph (28,000 km/h), it would take 166,000 years to reach it.

Time isn't the only problem. The journey wouldn't be possible because

Time lord
The Lord of Time is an enemy of the JLA. He is able to travel through time, and his goal is to conquer time and space.

Some scientists are trying to develop solar-sail powered spacecraft like this, which will capture the Sun's energy and use it to fuel journeys out of the Solar System.

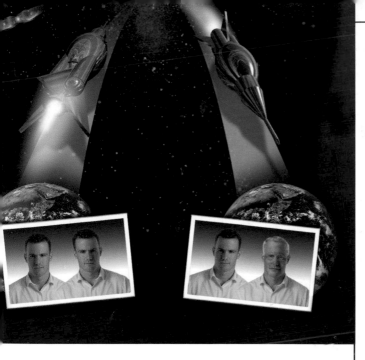

Strange things might happen if humans could travel close to light-speed. Five years might pass for one twin who journeys into space in a spacecraft, while 50 years pass for the twin who stays behind on Earth. When the journey ends, the Earth twin would be much older than the space traveler!

the shuttle couldn't carry the vast amount of food and rocket fuel needed to travel so far.

If human beings are to make it to the stars one day, scientists will have to invent a way of traveling at near light-speed, using little or no fuel. One idea is a spacecraft that won't need to carry its own fuel. Instead, it would have a huge solar sail and be pushed through space by the Sun's energy, in much the same way that wind blows a sailing ship.

Prankster
Qwsp is a silver-haired sprite from Zrfff, a place in the fifth dimension.

The Big Bang

War of the worlds
Not content with wiping out planets and plotting to demolish entire galaxies, the supervillain Imperiex hoped to create a black hole big enough to swallow the entire Universe!

The Universe isn't just huge, it's getting bigger all the time. Most scientists believe that it began about 13 billion years ago, when an infinitesimally hot and tiny speck of something suddenly exploded. This explosion is called the Big Bang, and it was the beginning of time, space, and everything!

The Big Bang was so powerful that in less than a second the Universe grew from smaller than an atom to bigger than a galaxy. It is still expanding today, with the galaxies speeding farther and farther away from each other. Humans may have figured out how and when the Universe began, but no one knows

The Big Bang was the biggest explosion there has ever been.

whether it will ever end. Most scientists think it will continue to expand forever. Others believe that one day the Universe may start shrinking and that eventually everything will crash together in a Big Crunch!

Early Universe
This image was taken by a satellite launched by NASA in 1990, and it shows what the Universe looked like about 300,000 years after the Big Bang. The blue areas are cooler clouds of gas.

Glossary

Algae
Life forms that range in size from a tiny single cell to seaweeds 160 feet (50 meters) long. Most algae live in water.

Asteroid
A rocky space body that orbits a star but is much smaller than a planet.

Astronomer
An expert in astronomy, the scientific study of space and space bodies such as stars, planets, and moons.

Atmosphere
A layer of gases that surrounds a planet or moon.

Atom
The smallest part of a chemical element such as hydrogen or oxygen.

Bacteria
Most bacteria are single-celled life forms that are so tiny that they can only be seen under a microscope.

Core
The innermost part of a star or planet.

Crater
A bowl-shaped hole in the ground left after a large space rock lands or a bomb explodes. The mouth of a volcano is also called a crater.

Diameter
The length of a straight line drawn from one side of a circle or ball shape through its center to the other side.

Infinitesimal
Extremely small.

Invisible
Something that cannot be seen.

Laser
A device that produces a very powerful, narrow beam of light, capable of cutting through metal and concrete.

Missile
A flying weapon such as a bomb.

Moon
A space body that orbits a planet. Unlike stars, moons cannot produce their own light. They appear to shine only when sunlight bounces off them.

NASA
Short for National Aeronautics and Space Administration, the US government agency that researches into and carries out space exploration.

Orbit
The path of one space body around another, more massive object.

Planet
A large, ball-shaped space body that orbits a star. Unlike stars, planets cannot produce their own light.

Radiation
A form of energy, such as light or radio waves.

Satellite
An object held in orbit around another, larger object by its gravity, such as a moon or spacecraft orbiting a planet.

Solar system
A star and all the space bodies trapped in orbit around the star by its gravity.

Star
A hot, shining, vast ball of gas, which produces heat and light energy in its core.

Telescope
An optical telescope is a device that, when you look through it, makes faraway objects appear larger. Radio telescopes collect invisible radio waves from space.

X-ray
A form of radiation that can pass through many substances that light cannot. Doctors use X-ray machines to take photographs of bones and teeth.